PROPERTY ™

G000165066

PROPERTY™
made simple

PETER STANLEY

Typeset in Trebuchet

Disclaimer

1. This guide is produced for general guidance only and professional advice should be sought before any decision is made. Individual circumstances can vary and therefore no responsibility can be accepted by the publisher Property Made Simple Ltd for any action taken, or any decision made to refrain from action, by any readers of this guide. If you do need professional advice, please contact the relevant professional body.

2. Tax rules and legislation are constantly changing and reference should be made to the prevailing legislation and regulations.

3. Property Made Simple Ltd do not offer financial, legal or investment advice. If you require such advice then, we urge you to seek the opinion of an appropriate professional in the relevant field. We care about your success and therefore urge you to take appropriate advice before you put any of your financial of other resources at risk.

4. Property values can fall as well as rise and any investment in property should be made for the medium to long term.

5. To the fullest extent permitted by law, Property Made Simple Ltd do not accept liability for any direct, indirect, special, consequential or other losses or damages of whatever kind arising from using this guide.

This guide is provided "as is" without express or implied warranty.

ACKNOWLEDGEMENTS

I'd like to thank all the property investors who spent time with me, on numerous occasions, patiently explaining the reasons why I should invest in property.

I must also thank those friends and ex-colleagues who helped and supported me during my decision to leave the nine to five and not least to my family for their constant patience and understanding.

Finally, I must thank Bookshaker.com for transforming my thoughts and ideas into a coherent and practical guide to investing in property.

CONTENTS

BUILD ON YOUR SUCCESS
ABOUT PETER STANLEY

PROPERTY MADE SIMPLE SERVICES

USEFUL RESOURCES

FOREWORD

Never could a book have arrived on my doorstep at a more opportune moment!

I am a fledgling property investor myself; I have one Buy to Let flat in London which I bought in the middle of 2004. Now, eighteen months later, my first ever tenant is vacating and I had some decisions to make about re-decorating, whether to renew or just clean carpets and so on. All the answers were in Peter's book, including a top tip I hadn't thought of myself about photographing my next tenant and collecting their National Insurance number. And a reminder about my overdue landlord's gas check.

This came as no surprise to me as I know Peter pretty well. How entirely appropriate that his book is full of down-to-earth, easy to read common sense, delivered with a lightness of touch – for such is the man.

Peter lays out how investing in property can make you a Millionaire in a surprisingly short few years. He is encouraging, and his text is fear-busting and jargon free. This is a great place to start if you think you would like to get into property but are teetering on the edge, curious and a little bit fearful.

It is also a reminder checklist for those of us who know a little bit, and you know what they say about a little knowledge? Well, we can make up for that by using Peter's comprehensive little book.

Property Made Simple explains how you too can learn to evaluate property as a great investment, and set up your portfolio to create passive income giving you freedom to live the life of your choice. Peter motivates his reader and elicits confidence. Hmm, perhaps we can all do this if we read, digest, learn, research, and dip a toe in the water. And perhaps it might be interesting as well as lucrative for us, and yes, perhaps it will even be fun?

This book is both comforting and empowering. When you are ready to start, it seems do-able. As Peter himself says, this book is not time-limited, nor will it self-destruct. If perchance you read it now and decide you are not ready, put it back on the shelf. I know you will go back to it. I know you will feel it calling to you from your library, for property is addictive. The maths is very sexy and I should know, I am an Accountant.

If not now, then the day will come when you realise that property investing is a no-brainer that makes much, much more than your day job and offers the chance to protect and underpin both your own future and that of your loved ones. What are YOU waiting for?

I can't think of anyone I'd rather "do" property with than Peter Stanley who is quite simply an expert with a modest and small e, but nonetheless a Top Bloke with a capital T and B.

I learned a lot from this book and I know I will return to it often.

Judith Morgan
www.judithmorgan.com
November 2005

THE BASICS

WHY PLAY THE PROPERTY INVESTING GAME?

When I was young I used to enjoy playing Monopoly.

However, we weren't allowed to put any houses or hotels on the board and I couldn't work out why.

Perhaps it was because the game would have taken too long or more likely because the arguments would have started sooner!

Everything would go well until the point at which one person owned most of the property on the board and the rest of us were living from one salary to the next.

Over time, I learned to buy as much property as possible and would borrow from the Bank when I was a bit short.

However, it took me many years to realise that the game was actually modelled on real life!

It took me even longer to start spending money on things that increase in value over time, rather than reducing in value!

So why invest in property?

- Job security no longer exists so an alternative income stream from property is a necessary safety net
- Pensions are no longer providing enough for retirement – so property might be a more reliable alternative investment
- To create a more financially certain future
- To provide an additional income stream
- To leave a valuable legacy for your children or loved ones
- It's easier to value than a portfolio of shares
- Low returns from bank deposit accounts require a higher growth investment
- You could get a return of £15k on an investment of £100k

THINK ABOUT IT...

If you had an extra £500 per month, how would you use it? Or, if you were given the equivalent of £10,000 in 5 years, what would you do with it?

BUT IT'S TOO LATE TO MAKE MONEY FROM PROPERTY...

I was recently talking with some friends about the news on TV and suggested starting a new news channel that had more *good* news.

Can you imagine the effect it would have if the late night news was uplifting, rather than the usually collection of doom and gloom?

We came to the conclusion that it wouldn't be popular, as strangely, most people tend to prefer hearing about bad news.

How many times have you heard somebody say that something's too good to be true, it will never last, or it's an accident waiting to happen?

Then again pessimists are rarely disappointed!

Perhaps these people are in training for the queue in the post office when they collect their pensions, to make sure that they're champion moaners!

Seriously though, if you had bought property 5 years ago, you could now be getting a £6,000 return per annum on an investment that had cost you just £45,000.

Today, that same property would cost you between £90,000 and £120,000!

So, of course it would have been better if you had bought already, but hindsight is always 20/20.

But the good news (if you can bear it) is that even if you haven't invested *yet*, it is still possible to buy properties that will show you a 7% income return on your money (without trying too hard) and that's discounting any capital growth.

While the number of properties has increased, the stigma of renting[1] has disappeared, which coupled with other factors, means that the size of the market has increased substantially.

---

[1] Renting used to be seen as only for the poor, with the majority of houses for rent being in working class areas, but the number and type of properties available to rent these days covers the whole spectrum of property.

WHAT THIS BOOK WILL SHOW YOU

This course will help to guide you through the property investment process by helping you to:

- Work out your investment strategy
- Breakthrough the jargon
- Research an area
- Appraise a property
- Understand how to fund the purchase
- Negotiate with the vendor
- Arrange any refurbishment work
- Find a tenant
- Review your progress

The course has been written with the UK market in mind, but the concepts and techniques apply to any country with a demand for rental property and where property is freely traded.

However, I must stress that there is no right way and no wrong way to invest in property, as it really depends upon your personal aims.

The basic purpose of property investing falls into 2 main categories:

1. Additional Income
2. Capital Growth

People who want an additional income will be carefully measuring the cash generated by their investment, looking for yields of over 7%.

They don't rely on increases in value, but see it as a bonus and their main aim is to generate a monthly income from their investment.

Conversely, there are people who don't want an extra income, perhaps because they are higher rate tax-payers, but instead want a longer term savings vehicle.

For them, they want the rent to cover the mortgage (the interest of which is tax deductible), but may accept a small shortfall, on the idea that the property will double in value every 7 years (or 4 years in the South East)[2]

It is possible to get a mix of the 2 strategies, but most people have a preference for one or the other.

THINK ABOUT IT...

Which strategy would make most sense to you – Extra Income or Capital Growth?

---

[2] Source ODPM (office of the deputy prime minister)

REASON OR EXCUSE?

There are a lot of myths surrounding investing in property; some founded in fact and some in fiction.

Most people who aren't investing in property come up with the same list of problems. But I quickly learned that they didn't want answers – just excuses for their lack of action.

I DON'T WANT TO FIX TOILETS / DO DIY

Who does? But tell me... when was the last time you fixed your *own* toilet at home?

I spent many weekends on my first property and while I gained a lot of knowledge and tools, I quickly realised that when I *had* to do it, it wasn't any fun. Now, I allow for the cost of labour when assessing deals, as this is a business, not a hobby.

I DON'T KNOW WHERE TO START

Just start at the very beginning.

Look at an area you know well, collect some sales particulars and compare them to a list of properties available for rent.

As you work through this book, simply keep an eye on your chosen area, sales prices and rental prices. Don't worry about how long it takes you to progress to the next stage, as it's not a race.

I HAVEN'T GOT THE TIME

Could you spare 30 minutes per week?

If not, then you should ask for a refund on this book, as you won't have the time to read it, let alone, get the benefit from it!

However, if you spend just 30 minutes a week researching, you'll soon find out if the property investment bug gets you.

I DON'T WANT TO DEAL WITH "PROBLEM TENANTS"

There *are* bad tenants out there, but there are also some very good ones.

Using an agent should reduce the risk, but if you are still uncomfortable, it is possible to take out insurance to cover any damage or lost rent.

Most landlords ask for a month's security deposit and for the first month's rent in advance, so this will provide some cushion in the event of a bad tenant.

Over the years, there are bound to be times when you have problems with tenants, but try to see it as one of the prices you pay for the rewards that property investing can bring about.

I use an agent because it makes my life a lot easier – I don't want telephone calls from tenants on a Saturday night, when I'm half way through my dinner.

I DON'T KNOW ANY TRADESMEN

There are plenty of good tradesmen, but finding reliable ones can be more difficult.

If you have time, you could meet them, but if not, your letting agent should have contacts. You could also ask friends, relatives and contacts who they know.

A referral is usually best, as you can see their work, but make sure you are comparing like with like. A builder who has rebuilt a garden wall may not be for the right person for building an extension.

PROPERTY INVESTING IS ONLY FOR THE RICH

You don't need a lot of money to invest in property and as you become more experienced, you'll learn ways of holding less and less cash in a property.

If the area you're looking at is too expensive then find somewhere else nearby that's cheaper.

THE BUBBLE HAS BURST

The next time that someone says this to you, politely ask what they're basing their opinion on.

Then you could move on to ask them how many properties *they* own. Most won't be investors, nor have they been investors.

If they talk about the slowdown in the housing market, the killer question is to ask about the rate of growth.

At the time of writing (2005) people are talking of a slowdown, yet the Halifax are reporting single digit growth, down from double digit growth.

Put another way, this means that prices will increase between 5% and 9% per annum. The best bit though, is that you get this return on the purchase price, not on your investment.

So if you buy a £100,000 house, with £15,000 investment, your property will increase at between £5000 and £9000 per annum, as well as any monthly income!

THINK ABOUT IT...

What, if anything, scares you about investing in property and what can you do to allay your fears?

JARGON BUSTING

People love to use jargon, for 3 main reasons:

- They can use less words
- It makes them look like they know what they're talking about
- It makes them feel "in the know"

When I worked in a bank, we used to shorten most things into TLAs (three letter acronyms) and one Christmas, just for fun, someone composed a whole story, purely of TLAs.

The really sad part was that it made perfect sense to me!

I realised that as soon as you learn the lingo of any area, you can convince people you're an expert, even though you only know the jargon.

I've listed some commonly used jargon you're likely to come across below.

Yield – the return on your investment, like an interest rate on a bank deposit or a dividend on a share – Usually expressed as a percentage.

Capital Growth – increases in the value of the property.

Passive Income – money that comes from an investment, without your direct involvement – as opposed to a salary.

AST – assured short-hold tenancy agreement, usually for a period of 6 or 12 months.

Fixed, floating and capped mortgages – covered in detail in the finance section.

Stamp Duty – a tax payable to the government on purchase of a property.

OPM (Other People's Money) – using the money of other people (e.g. a bank and a tenant) for the purchase and repayment.

OPT (Other People's Time) – Putting other people's time and skills to work for you such as using a letting agent, builderetc.

Leverage – I'll go into leverage in more detail later, but using your initial 15% deposit, will enable you to get a return based on 100% of the cost of the asset.

So, you leverage your £15,000 deposit to earn capital growth on a £100,000 investment.

RECAP

We've made some good progress so far on your journey to becoming a property investor.

We've talked about the reasons for investing in property and the key principles.

We've blown away some of the common problems (which are nothing more than excuses), that your friends and acquaintances are guaranteed to remind you of.

We've looked at some of the jargon to increase your confidence and help you in your discussions with property people and financiers.

By now, you're probably also looking at the property pages of the local newspaper and have been taking an interest in the local house prices and properties for sale.

So you're taking your first steps to building your property empire!

Don't worry if this seems scary, as we'll take it at a manageable pace and break it down into bite size chunks, to make the whole process easy.

THINK ABOUT IT...

Take a few moments to reread this first chapter to allow the information to sink in. Think about what you want to get out of property investing and what you're willing to put in.

STARTING POINT

FEELING CONFIDENT?

So you're still keen to learn some more about investing in property.

Perhaps you're feeling a little nervous. Don't. This isn't one of those double glazing deals where you have to make your purchase within 48 hours. You're in control and you can dictate the pace.

So, let's take the next step and have a good look at where you are right now.

Now, if you're the kind of person who just likes to get on with it and take action, then try to bear with me. You'll pick up some useful tips in this and the coming chapters that will serve you well when you spring into action.

SP simply means – what's your Situation at Present.

I don't mean geographically, but how are you feeling right now? How quickly do you want to invest? How prepared do you feel? What's your confidence level?

However, the key point is not to worry about your starting point, but to focus on where you're going.

With persistence any obstacles can be overcome. Nothing, and I mean nothing, can stop you from investing in property if you want it badly enough.

Remember, this is a journey and that unlike most of your friends and colleagues, you're taking steps to get there.

It took me over 5 years to move from thinking about investing in property to *actually* buying my first place. Over this time, I saw values increase substantially, but I wanted to wait until I was ready and had done my research.

THINK ABOUT IT...

How long do you think it will be before you've bought your first property?

WHAT'S YOUR MOTIVATION?

This may seem like a daft question, but it's really important.

When you've just missed out on a deal, or have seen 10 properties and all of them are rubbish, or when everyone's telling you that the bubble has burst, you'll need to know the answer to this question.

Put simply, why do you want to invest in property?

If you don't know, take some time to think.

Buy yourself a scrapbook for your property investing journey and write the answer in it. The book needn't be expensive, just something that will work as a notepad, aide memoir and journal.

SO WHY DID I GET INVOLVED?

I used to work for one of the high street banks and over the years I noticed that the people who were wealthy had property. So I started to talk to these investors and find out more.

These people were borrowing money to buy property and the rent that they charged not only covered the mortgage payments, but left some spare, as income, for them.

But what got me fired up was when I realised that the lender didn't want *any* of the increase in the value of the property. They were happy as long as their interest was paid.

So with my £15,000, I could buy a £100,000 property and I got to benefit from the increase on that £100,000, provided that I paid the bank around 6% per annum.

I wanted to earn enough passive income to be able to give up my day job and be a full time investor.

Passive income's like having a job, but without the hard work, so the money comes to you even while you're, sleeping, on holiday, enjoying a hobby and generally spending your time as you wish.

If you work it just right then you can build your passive income to a level where you never need to work again! Now wouldn't that be great?

Can you imagine working for the fun of it, because the money side was already taken care of?

I know it seems like a tall order and I'm not there yet, but I'm closer today than I was this time last year and I'll be closer still in a year's time.

Even knowing why you're doing this, there will still be times when you doubt your calling, so keep the journal close to hand.

THINK ABOUT IT...

Why are you doing this?

Perhaps you want to...

- Provide for your retirement, so you can grow old disgracefully.
- Have someone else pay for your holiday home.
- Generate an extra income to enjoy a better quality of life.
- Save for your children's/grandchildren's education.
- Sit on a beach, somewhere nice and sunny, for more than 2 weeks a year.
- Tell the boss what you *really* think of him at your next appraisal.

SELF BELIEF - CAN I REALLY DO IT?

We've just looked at the possible reasons for investing in property and thought about our reasons for taking action.

The next step is to think about our self-belief.

Given the right support and knowledge, can you turn the motivation into action?

On a scale of 1 to 10, how confident do you feel?

If you scored less than 7 then let's take some time to consider the reasons and think about what we can do to improve your confidence.

If you feel that you don't yet know enough to take action then I can assure you that this book will give you more than enough information to get yourself on the property investment ladder.

More than that, once you are *on* the ladder, it will help you to take steps up the ladder.

We will also work through the process in easily digestible chunks so that you don't feel overwhelmed.

You should also remember that this isn't a race. Whether you buy a property next month, next year, or 10 years from now, the principles I'm sharing will work.

This book won't self-destruct after one reading, so come back to the sections you're unsure about, until you feel that you've mastered them.

Seek out experienced property investors and spend time with them. There are a number of organisations catering for landlords. The Residential Landlords Association (www.rla.org.uk) is one and they hold regular meetings.

Apart from providing you with access to a large network of contacts, it will reinforce your learning, build your confidence and make you realise that you know enough to get started.

THINK ABOUT IT...

On a scale of 1 to 10, how strong is my self belief? What could I do to improve it?

WHAT'S YOUR INVESTING STRATEGY?

Let's take some time to think about your strategy.

If we compare your property investing to a journey, then you'll realise that you need to know where you're headed to make sure that you end up where you want to be.

As I mentioned earlier, property portfolios generally split into 2 camps; either capital growth or income.

Capital Growth properties provide little income over the short to medium term, but a substantial uplift in value over the same period.

Income properties provide a nice level of income over the short to medium term, with a typically lower uplift in value.

In reality, most properties are somewhere between the two, but have a leaning to one type of income or the other.

Having looked at your motivation already, you'll be able to judge which type would suit you best. The next step is to look at the type of properties that will provide you with what you're looking for.

Capital growth tends to occur in more affluent areas, as more people want to live in those areas over time.

Income tends to be in the lower socio-economic areas, at the cheaper end of the rental market, where yields of up to 15% are possible. Rents aren't directly proportional to the value of a property, so the rent for a cheaper property is a higher percentage of it's value than an expensive house.

Areas of high capital growth often produce little income over the short to medium term, as is often the case in parts of London.

So, you need to think about whether you want an ongoing income stream, spread over a number of properties or an increasing asset base that may provide little by way of income over the next 5-10 years, but will give a good lump sum at the end.

For example, future university fees could be financed by an income-producing portfolio or by the sale of a property that had increased in value, using the equity released.

THINK ABOUT IT...

What kind of property am I looking for - Capital growth or income?

WHERE TO BUY

Many people get hung up on this point, as they seem to think that there is a particular place that they should buy.

Sometimes, their fear of getting it wrong prevents them from taking *any* action at all.

Now, there are places that are more likely to give you problems, but that's not the key issue here.

For your first property, avoid the hype of so called property hot spots, for the simple reasons that they are hot in someone's opinion and often, if you've heard about them from the media then you're already too late.

Don't worry about spotting the next big area either. You can take those kind of risks when you've got more properties under your belt.

Start off with areas that you know well and assess them against your strategy and target market. If your local area is too expensive then think about other places that you know well and are relatively near, for example a nearby city or where a friend lives.

Then consider the rental income compared to the interest on the mortgage – simply take the loan amount, multiply it by the interest rate, expressed as a percentage and divide it by 12 to get the monthly interest payment. For example:

100,000 x 6% = £6,000 per year (£500 per month)

Again, people think that there is a magical figure or yield for this equation, but it's a matter of personal choice.

For example, if your goal is to get good capital growth, you may be happy to pay something towards the mortgage from your own pocket.

Conversely, if you want income, you will want to maximise the cash you get out of the deal on a monthly basis by ensuring the rent you charge is higher than the rental income figure you work out.

THINK ABOUT IT...

Use the Ideal Property Checklist on the next page to assess your chosen area and some real properties you're looking at against your investment strategy. If you'd like to print off extra copies of this checklist then download it (along with other useful tools) at *www.wealthaudit.com/property*. If a property meets the requirement score it a 1, if it doesn't score it a zero. The properties with the highest scores most closely match your requirements.

IDEAL PROPERTY CHECKLIST

Requirements	e.g.	1	2	3	4
Location	1				
Target Market	0				
Number of Bedrooms	1				
Garden	1				
Parking	0				
Off-road parking	0				
Through lounge	1				
Public transport	1				
Neighbours	1				
Schools	1				
Rent per month	1				
Purchase price	0				
No work required	1				
Return	1				
Score (out of 14)	10				

LOCAL KNOWLEDGE

Once you've looked at a couple of areas, you'd be wise to hone in on a square mile of your chosen area.

By doing this, you'll be able to keep up to date with the local prices, keep in contact with the local agents and will even be able to read the notes in your local post office.

It helps to pick up a copy of the local newspaper too, as this will tell you about any good news or bad news affecting the area. Some areas may have their own website, which will save you the journey.

Call in at the local shop and talk to them about the area – you'll be amazed what they know, but try to pick a quiet time.

Local knowledge will also help you when talking with vendors, as many people prefer not to sell their home to investors.

While there is a temptation to look at a broad area, this tactic makes it hard to be an expert and translates into being a jack of all trades – master of none.

You'll soon realise that there are great disparities within even such a small area, but with your knowledge, you'll know the market inside out.

You can use this knowledge to know whether the factor that reduces a house price for sale will also affect the rental income that could be made from the same property.

Never underestimate the power of local knowledge.

RECAP

In this chapter, we looked at your reasons for taking action and the strength of your self belief as a starting point. After that, we took some time to think about the kind of property you're looking for. I've seen too many people get distracted by "good deals" that don't match their investment strategy.

People are also often caught by the "big deal syndrome". For example, they may decide to look for a one bedroom flat, but in their research, they find a block of 6 self-contained apartments and want to buy them all!

While the flats, individually, would meet their criteria, the extra resources, time and money required can overwhelm the novice!

Then we moved into the real action and looked at where we should start our research, followed by assessing some real life examples (using the Ideal

Property Checklist), which we thought would meet our investment criteria.

Using this information, you've narrowed down your patch and have looked at ways of keeping up to date with the local market and any issues that will positively or negatively impact on the value of local property.

Now that we've established a solid foundation for your property empire, I'm sure you'll be feeling confident as we move onto the first steps in building it.

PETER STANLEY

FIRST STEPS

SYSTEMS

I know that some people love systems, with checklists, graphs and even different colours for different things.

Sadly, I'm not one of those people. I prefer to keep most of the information in my head and do my calculations on the back of a beer-mat.

However, I've learned that having systems in place offers a number of advantages:

- You get to spend more time on the creative stuff rather than simply keeping track of things.
- You can compare 2 properties quickly, in different areas.
- You can assess the work required on a property, it's sale value and the resulting profit in minutes.
- You can calculate the level of mortgage that a property will support, based on the rental income.
- You get to know about every property that will be sold by auction in your chosen areas
- You increase your knowledge on a weekly basis

Einstein had a theory that he didn't want to clutter his brain with unnecessary things, so as to keep it free for creating. Once when asked for his phone number, he looked it up in a phone directory, as he didn't think it was worth remembering.

If you're not careful it's easy to become overloaded with information, but the use of systems will reduce this problem.

Some examples are:

- A Property Appraisal Sheet to analyse deals –(see the resources section at the back of this book).
- A Prospecting Letter (see the resources section at the back of this book).
- A list of the local estate agents, with a checklist for when you last visited them.
- An Ideal Property Checklist, to reduce the time you spend looking at estate agent's brochures.
- Regularly reading the local newspaper
- Reading the property section of a weekend broadsheet

I realise that this may seem like a lot of work, but I find that it saves me a lot of time when analysing deals, which frees me up and reduces the hassle factor.

THINK ABOUT IT...

What systems would make your life easier? Visit *www.wealthaudit.com/property* for downloads of tools and templates specifically designed for property investors.

YOUR SUPPORT TEAMS

Now this is an important part of growing your property empire.

You need 2 support teams:

1. A property support team
2. A personal support team

Do you remember when you first learned to ride a bicycle – it's a long time ago for me – so it's a bit hazy.

You probably started off with a three wheeler, then progressed to your first two wheeler, with stabilisers. After that I guess you moved to your first bike without stabilisers then to something bigger with a few gears and then to something full size with lots of gears.

At the start, I'm sure that you were shown how it worked, having probably been pushed along by an adult. Then you may have ridden around for a while with stabilisers.

When they came off for the first, you probably had someone older with you to make sure you didn't fall off.

It's just the same with property. You need people to make sure that you don't skip the first stages and go straight to a full size racing bike. It might be great for a while, but the crashes can be spectacular.

For your property team, find some people who've been there already and know the ropes. Ideally they'll have a couple of properties and can help you through the process.

If you don't know anyone then ask your friends who they know or join an association such as the Residential Landlords Association (see www.rla.org.uk) or National Landlords Association (www.landlords.org.uk).

Find a letting agent and estate agent in your target area who you like and respect, but who will spend some time with you and answer your questions.

Secondly and just as importantly, get a team of people around you who will provide personal support through this learning process. They don't need to know about property, but do need to be supportive of both you and your ideas.

However, be sure that they're not the kind of people who will be negative and don't take any property advice from the second group, as they're likely to know far less than you do!

I've been lucky as my 2 groups overlap.

I also find that I will talk to particular people about the technical aspects of a deal and others about the negotiation or people side, depending on their own personal strengths.

For example, I may need someone analytical to help with structuring a deal, but other times I'll need a great people-person to help with the negotiation.

Even when you're more experienced at investing, you'll need people with the sticking plasters. I remember the first time I pulled a wheelie, it was great for the first 20 feet, until I went over the back of the bike!

THINK ABOUT IT...

Who do you want in your support team?

READING

Up until about two years ago, I used to hate reading, as I read so many documents and emails at work, that by the time I came home I had reached overload.

One day, I realised that whatever I wanted to do, someone else had not only been there before me, but had written a book on it. By reading it I could learn from *their* successes and avoid some of their mistakes.

I also found books that suited my style of reading and concentrated on those types of books that resonated with me.

Then I found out about ezines[3], which are electronic magazines, that arrive in your email inbox after you've signed up for them.

I read them most weeks, but other times I simply skim through them and at the moment, I'm signed up to about 4 ezines, covering a range of subjects.

---

[3] If you haven't already then why not sign up for my ezine at www.propertymadesimple.com?

Then there are forums, where people talk about property and business ideas, which I use to keep abreast of developments and to look for deals.

There are also a number of good landlords associations offering good advice and reference information, from what to do with a bad tenant, to advice on issuing an assured short hold tenancy (AST).

BOOKS I LIKE...

- The Richest Man in Babylon by George Clason
- Who Moved My Cheese by Dr Spencer Johnson
- Fish! by Stephen Lundin
- Rich Dad, Poor Dad by Robert Kiyosaki
- Think and Grow Rich by Napoleon Hill
- How To Win Friends and Influence People by Dale Carnegie
- The One Minute Millionaire by Mark Victor Hansen
- From Rags to Riches Through Real Estate by Russ Whitney
- Synchronicity by Joseph Jaworski

EZINES AND WEBSITES I LIKE...

- www.burg.com
- www.singingpig.co.uk
- www.jimrohn.com
- www.upyourstreet.com
- www.philiphumbert.com
- www.multimap.co.uk
- www.rightmove.com

TIMESCALES

People move at different speeds.

Some like to be in the fast lane and once they've learned something new, they're off to put it into action.

Others like to ponder and consider the information, before thinking about the ramifications of action against non-action.

The merits of each camp are clear, as are the disadvantages.

However, the key point is this. It doesn't matter which camp you're in as long as you make sure that you work in a way that suits you.

Normally, I'm the kind of guy that hates the planning process and can't abide people who want to talk rather than do. I've slowed down a little as I've got older, but I still hate planning meetings that don't produce an action plan!

With that in mind, you may be surprised to hear that I spent 5 years researching the local market and weighing up the merits of property investment doing my first deal.

I put this down to my training as a bank manager, which meant that I wanted to eradicate *all* of the risk, rather than looking at ways of minimising it, or looking at solutions to any potential problems.

It would be easy to regret not having invested earlier, given the subsequent price rises, but I simply wasn't in the right place for property investing and so my decision to keep looking was right for me then.

By the time I invested, I knew the local market inside out, had my support teams in place and knew my strategy inside out which paid off.

So, don't worry if you aren't ready to jump in yet as the principles will apply for many years to come.

THINK ABOUT IT...

How long is a realistic timescale for you to move on your first property investment?

LEARNING

To use the analogy of riding a bicycle again, some things need to be learned by doing them rather than talking or reading about them.

You can't learn to ride a bike in a classroom. You have to go out and get on a bike.

Sometimes you're going to scrape your knees but the trick is making sure that you don't do any serious damage!

So, using your Ideal Property Checklist (downloadable at *www.wealthaudit.com/property*) , go and look at some properties.

Find a couple of houses or flats in your target area that meet your criteria and book appointments to see them.

If you're nervous then find a friend to go with you for moral support. I bet you can think of the ideal person as you're reading this!

Try testing your powers of observation and leave the sales papers in the car while looking round the property. This will give you the time to talk to the vendor, so you can find out why they're selling and ask other pertinent questions.

It also means that you'll have to stop for a coffee or a drink afterwards to write up the notes!

Don't let the estate agent push you for a decision, simply tell them that you liked the house, but have a few other properties to see and will call them in a couple of days. You could also say that you liked the house but are just finding your feet with the local market.

You can then use these real life examples when we look at the section on buying and negotiating in later chapters. Just make sure you don't get carried away and start making offers!

THINK ABOUT IT...

Which properties have you seen that would suit your criteria and when can you see them?

RESEARCH

Armed with your local paper and local knowledge, you're now on the look out for properties that meet your criteria.

Remember that we're not ready to buy yet, so don't get too excited or carried away and start making offers. There will always be other good deals just around the corner.

Don't be tempted to skip this part of the book, as you will learn some invaluable lessons about people, property and yourself.

Now that you're moving closer to the buying stage and have a better idea of what you're looking for, you'll probably be seeing your target area in a different light.

Before you book appointments to look inside a property, take a good look at the outside and use the Ideal Property Checklist to judge/assess what work needs to be done. This will give you a ballpark figure, which can be fine-tuned after you've been inside.

Don't worry about spotting everything, just look for the major things, like the condition of the windows, the state of the roof and guttering.

Take a guess at what you think the property is worth.

Again, don't worry about being exact, but use it as an opportunity to hone your local knowledge.

Once you've looked at the outside of the property, re-read the estate agent's particulars, reading between the lines, to notice what they're really saying.

Common phrases include:

- In need of modernisation
- Would suit first time buyer or investor
- Close to motorway network
- Great opportunity

I'm sure that once you've *seen* the property, you'll more fully understand the meaning of these phrases!

THINK ABOUT IT...

Go out and look at some properties, using the Ideal Property Checklist.

RECAP

So now we're starting to make some visible progress.

We're using the foundation that we built in the first 2 chapters and have started to take some action.

You'll have thought about the systems you need to help make decisions and save time as you build your portfolio.

You've probably also started to recruit people into your support teams.

We've looked at some useful books to read, websites that will help you assess an area and some ezines to help you on your journey.

You've also thought about the timescales for your first investment property and we've dispelled the myth that you need to take action immediately.

Then we moved into the real action part, where you'll have looked at some real properties and used the Ideal Property Checklist to assess the property.

Now we've started looking it's time to work out how you're going to pay for your property.

PETER STANLEY

FINANCE MADE SIMPLE

GENERAL PRINCIPLES

Many people have a blind spot when it comes to finance, thinking it's more complicated than it really is.

While my years in the Banking industry gave me an insight into it's workings, it was only when I read Robert Kiyosaki's, *Rich Dad, Poor Dad* that I learned how to use bank finance to buy assets and, more importantly, the distinction between assets and liabilities.

Perhaps it's because in British society, we think it's impolite to discuss money, so people take to showing their wealth in other ways – cars, house, clothes etc.

During my time at the Bank, I saw many people who appeared outwardly wealthy, but in fact, had minimal net assets.

Recently, I went to one of those free property seminars, as I'm a sucker for anything that's free – and was amazed to hear people quoting property portfolios of £1 million, but with less than £100,000 equity.

While this may seem scary at first, they know that property usually doubles in value every 7 years, which means that they will be millionaires in 2012.

The secret to borrowing money is to make sure that it *earns* you more than it *costs* you. For a property investor, this means that your tenant pays more in rent, than you pay for the mortgage.

The real breakthrough comes when you realise that the banks and building societies really want to lend you the money, you just need to know the rules of the game.

In this chapter, you will learn the rules of the game, assess your attitude to risk and be able to break through the jargon used in the finance industry.

THINK ABOUT IT...

At what level of borrowing would you start to get scared – £100,000, £500,000, £1 million or £10 million?

TYPES OF DEBT

There are many different ways of funding your property investment and during the next few pages, we'll look at the advantages and disadvantages of each...

BANK/BUILDING SOCIETY DEBT

This is the most common form of financing property investment. People approach the Bank or Building Society, complete an application form and the Bank provides the loan.

EQUITY RELEASE

If the value of your home has risen since you bought it, you may be able to borrow some of the increased value. Usually this is done with the existing lender, but can be done with *any* financial institution.

Some people prefer to remortgage the property instead, to release funds.

BRIDGING FINANCE

This is similar to Bank finance, but is usually for a much shorter period (1 month to 12 months) and is much more expensive.

CREDIT CARDS

Given the competition in the credit card market (and the current 0% interest deals), this can be a cheap way of borrowing, but must only be used by people who are very disciplined.

INVESTOR

You may know someone with spare cash, who's looking for a good return on it.

Perhaps, they would like to invest in property, but don't have the knowledge, time or an understanding to get involved directly.

On the basis that you will be providing the time and effort, with their finance, you can come to an agreement on the split of profit.

CASH RESOURCES

Perhaps you have a pot of cash that you could invest yourself.

While this may seem the cheapest option, you should factor in the interest that you could have earned, from a "high" interest account.

THINK ABOUT IT...

Which type of finance would suit your circumstances best?

BANK DEBT

Banks like to lend for property.

They can see where their money is going, it can be valued easily and they have an asset to sell if you default. They can also pass off the legal risks to your solicitor and the building risks to the surveyor.

Given that they have the security of a property to fall back on, this is a relatively cheap form of finance.

Most lenders will advance a percentage of the value, from 60% to 85%, as long as interest is more than covered by rental income.

There are many different types of mortgage, but the main ones are...

CAPITAL & INTEREST

You make regular payments over the term of the loan, to repay the initial amount, plus interest on the amount borrowed.

INTEREST ONLY

You pay interest on the loan, but at the end of the term you will still owe the amount you originally borrowed.

This suits people who believe that the property will increase in value or people who want to keep their outgoings to a minimum.

We then move onto the basis on which interest is calculated:

VARIABLE RATE

This type of mortgage is linked to the base rate, with any changes in the Bank of England base rate being passed on to you, the borrower.

FIXED RATE

At the start of the loan, you decide on a period that you'd like to fix the interest rates for, after which it usually reverts to the lender's standard variable rate.

The term of the fixed rate is usually much shorter than the period of the loan and can range from 12 months to 10 years.

This type of mortgage is good for people who want to be certain of their interest costs, for a set period of time.

CAPPED RATE

Similar to a fixed rate, in that you know your maximum interest costs, but any reductions in base rate are passed onto you.

If this seems confusing then speak to a mortgage broker to advise you.

THINK ABOUT IT...

Which type of mortgage would suit you best? Get some professional advice here from a mortgage broker.

EQUITY RELEASE / CASH RESOURCES

I would imagine that the value of your home has increased substantially over the last couple of years. One way of raising cash is to borrow against this increased value, which is known as releasing the equity in your home.

At the risk of stating the obvious, this will increase your monthly outgoings and should be taken into account when assessing your monthly expenditure.

However, this can be a cheap way to borrow, as the interest rate will be the same, or near your mortgage rate.

It can also be a good time to reassess your mortgage interest rate, as it could be better to refinance your existing mortgage, to take advantage of the current mortgage offers.

When looking at releasing equity, lenders will usually lend up to 80% of the total value of your home, so to calculate the equity that can be released, simply subtract your existing mortgage from 80% of the total value.

On the other hand, you may have cash resources in a high interest bank or some shares that haven't been performing very well over the last couple of years.

While you may have enough money to buy a property outright, the power of leverage makes it more prudent to use the cash as a deposit for more than one property and to borrow the rest.

Here's a calculation of a worked example.

The Power of Leverage

£100,000 used to buy 1 house

Year	Income	Value
1	£ 6,000	£ 100,000
2	£ 6,000	£ 108,000
3	£ 6,300	£ 115,560
4	£ 6,300	£ 123,649
5	£ 6,615	£ 132,305
6	£ 6,615	£ 141,566
7	£ 6,946	£ 151,476
8	£ 6,946	£ 162,079
9	£ 7,293	£ 173,424
10	£ 7,293	£ 185,564
Total	**£ 66,308**	**£ 85,564**

£100,000 used to buy 6 houses

per house

Year	Income		Interest		Surplus		Value	
1	£	6,000	£	5,100	£	900	£	100,000
2	£	6,000	£	5,100	£	900	£	108,000
3	£	6,300	£	5,100	£	1,200	£	115,560
4	£	6,300	£	5,100	£	1,200	£	123,649
5	£	6,615	£	5,100	£	1,515	£	132,305
6	£	6,615	£	5,100	£	1,515	£	141,566
7	£	6,946	£	5,100	£	1,846	£	151,476
8	£	6,946	£	5,100	£	1,846	£	162,079
9	£	7,293	£	5,100	£	2,193	£	173,424
10	£	7,293	£	5,100	£	2,193	£	185,564
Total	**£**	**66,308**	**£**	**51,000**	**£**	**15,308**	**£**	**85,564**

For 6 properties

Year	Income	Interest	Surplus	Value
1	£ 36,000	£ 30,600	£ 5,400	£ 600,000
2	£ 36,000	£ 30,600	£ 5,400	£ 648,000
3	£ 37,800	£ 30,600	£ 7,200	£ 693,360
4	£ 37,800	£ 30,600	£ 7,200	£ 741,895
5	£ 39,690	£ 30,600	£ 9,090	£ 793,828
6	£ 39,690	£ 30,600	£ 9,090	£ 849,396
7	£ 41,675	£ 30,600	£ 11,075	£ 908,854
8	£ 41,675	£ 30,600	£ 11,075	£ 972,473
9	£ 43,758	£ 30,600	£ 13,158	£ 1,040,546
10	£ 43,758	£ 30,600	£ 13,158	£ 1,113,385
Total	**£ 397,845**	**£ 306,000**	**£ 91,845**	**£ 513,385**

Assumptions
6% interest rate, deposit of £15k per property,
£10k remaining
8% annual increase in house prices

THINK ABOUT IT...

How much equity do you have in your home and would you want to increase the debt against it?

BRIDGING FINANCE & CREDIT CARDS

Bridging finance is designed for short term financing, pending either a sale or longer term financing.

Bankers use a judgement on risk to measure their reward, which is why mortgages are cheaper than credit cards. They also use it to justify charging higher interest rates when people find it harder to borrow using standard finance.

Bridging finance is similar to a mortgage in that it's secured against a property, but is usually for a shorter term, agreed more quickly and consequently more expensive. Typical interest rates are between 1% and 2% a month, sometimes with a 1% entry and/or exit fee.

So borrowing £50,000 will cost you £1,000 per month!

If you know of a £75,000 property that can be bought for £60,000, you'll be buying at £15,000 below its market value.

Perhaps all your cash is already committed, so the only way that you can raise the money is by using bridging finance. Whilst this is an expensive way to borrow money, at around 2% per month, you may consider the monthly interest cost of £1,200 to be worthwhile as it allows you to get a £15,000 discount.

If those numbers didn't make you swallow hard, then you either saw the big picture or didn't read it properly!

The lending criteria for bridging loans are less strict than for normal debt, but be sure to know your escape route, as this type of debt can quickly swallow all of your profit!

Credit cards can be another source of short-term finance, and can be very cheap, if you take advantage of the balance transfer rates.

Be careful though, if you transfer the balance to another card, you must make sure that you don't run up debt on the first card.

Both of these methods are only for the very brave, disciplined and financially literate.

THINK ABOUT IT...

Do you think that this type of finance for you?

JARGON BUSTING

Most people use jargon like verbal shorthand, but I've known many people show their ignorance by using the words incorrectly.

If I don't know what someone means by a particular word, I ask. It teaches me something new and the tone of their response often gives me an insight into their personality.

There are enough financiers, solicitors and letting agents around to mean that you don't have to deal with people who annoy you. This is *your* business, so *you* get to decide who you deal with and who you don't!

So now you know about the different kinds of finance and what the lenders are looking for.

While many may use a credit scoring system to assess a loan, this is simply an automated version of **PARTS**:

- **P**urpose – What's the cash to be used for?
- **A**mount – Also what proportion is the loan of the total cost
- **R**epayment – When and how will they get their money back
- **T**erms – What interest rate, fees and insurance
- **S**ecurity – What happens if we don't get repaid

When you apply the above questions to property lending, the answers are fairly simple.

Yield – sometimes called return, but simply the rent/purchase price.

Flipping – selling a property for a profit, shortly after purchase.

Valuation Survey – simply that!

Homebuyer's Survey – provides more detailed information on the state of the property.

Full Structural Survey – all singing and dancing report, but quite expensive.

Timber and Damp Survey – will check the woodwork for signs of wet/dry rot etc.

Debt Capacity – it's possible to calculate the debt that a property will stand, using:

$$\frac{\text{Annual Rent}}{130\%^{*} \text{ x Interest Rate}}$$

---

* The ratio that the lender wants the interest covered by will vary from 100% to 130%, so make sure you ask them for their criteria.

Subject to the answer being less than 85% of the property value.

For example, if a property is worth £100,000, then the maximum that you could borrow would be £85,000.

However, if the monthly rent was £400, giving an annual rent of £4,800 and the interest rate was 6%, then the debt capacity would be:

$$\frac{4800}{130\% \times 6\%} = \text{£}61,538$$

If it were £600 per month, then the debt capacity would be

$$\frac{7200}{130\% \times 6\%} = \text{£}92,307 \quad \text{(subject to the max of 85\% – £85k)}$$

THINK ABOUT IT...

Are there any other phrases that you don't understand?

RECAP

So far, we've established what the Banks look for when assessing a deal.

We also know that they want to lend money for property and that they have clear guidelines on how much they will lend. Trust me property is one of the easiest things to get money for.

We now know their criteria for assessing a lending proposition, which means that we can answer any questions before they are asked.

We've also looked at the types of finance available and hopefully by now, you'll have thought about which type works best for you.

You may have even looked at some of the mortgages on offer, to see what the costs (interest rates and fees) are.

I hope that this chapter has shown you that finance is a very logical and straightforward part of buying property.

Of course, you'll increase the amount of debt you have, but unlike moving to a bigger home, this debt will not only be paid for by someone else, but will also give you an appreciating asset.

Now doesn't that make more sense than a new car?

However, the bit I really like is that you get the capital growth on the total value of the property, not just the 15% you've invested!

Now that we know how we're going to pay for our property, let's look at the buying process.

THE BUYING PROCESS

GENERAL PRINCIPLES OF BUYING

I know that you've probably been dying to get to this part, but believe me, you'll need to apply all of the lessons you've learnt so far, to be successful.

Make sure that your property empire is built on a firm foundation.

Buying a property to rent is completely different to buying your own home.

Things that may be important for a home are irrelevant when looking at investments as many add neither value nor increase the rental income.

Some examples of things that aren't important are:

- South facing gardens
- Nice decoration to your taste
- Luxury bathroom suites or kitchens
- Backwater location

Furthermore, as this is a numbers game, you will become less interested in paying extra because you like the vendor, or because the property is one of a kind or for some other subjective reason.

You'll soon realise that a lick of paint, new curtains, lampshades and maybe a new carpet can transform even the worst looking rooms. As much as I hate to admit it, the TV programmes that talk about neutral colour schemes are right.

So, when you're looking at a property, train your eye to see past the decoration, either good or bad and look at the rent you'll get compared to the purchase price, added to any tidying up costs.

One of the key mistakes that first time investors make is to make the property good enough for themselves to live in.

I'm strongly against slums, but a clean, tidy house in good repair will rent as well as one with all the latest mod cons - unless you're after the executive market.

THINK ABOUT IT...

What would you look for in a new home and would any of these factors increase the rental income?

WHO'S YOUR TARGET BUYER?

When you're looking to buy a house, it's easy to drown in information.

For the people who love information, it's easy to become bogged down in analysis paralysis, spending time creating graphs, spreadsheets and making endless comparisons.

Other people feel like they're drowning in paper and find themselves shutting down, unable to cope with any more property talk.

One way to prevent this is to spend time thinking about the type of tenant that you want.

There are 7 broad categories

1. Students
2. Singles
3. Couples or groups of friends
4. Families
5. Young professionals
6. Executive type lets
7. Retirement lets

As you can imagine, each of these types has distinct needs, problems and budgets and only a very few properties will cater for more than a couple of these categories at the same time.

So, you need to think about which type of tenant you want to attract and ensure that you *only* consider properties that meet *their* criteria.

However, initially it may be easier to consider what kind of tenants you *don't* want.

If you don't know what kind of tenants would suit an area, find a local letting agent and pick their brains.

THINK ABOUT IT...

Who would be your ideal tenant and who would be your worst nightmare?

HOW TO BUY - ESTATE AGENTS

While there are many ways to buy a property other than through an estate agent, it is the most common way.

By now, you'll have identified a particular area where you want to buy and will have driven around, or even better, walked the area.

You'll have been watching the prices over the last couple of weeks and will have a good idea of the nice bits and not so nice bits.

You may even have registered with a couple of estate agents to get property details as they come up.

The next step is to book an appointment with them.

Yes, I know that you're already on their mailing list, but you're off their radar.

The aim of the meeting is to let them know that you want to buy a house in the next couple of weeks and that you're a serious investor – your message will be strengthened if you ask about a couple of properties they're selling.

Tell them what you're looking for, but be very specific, as this will show that you're a serious investor and makes their life easier. It will also make you more recognisable when you ring up. Try to ask for the same person, so you can establish rapport.

When you're with them, ask them what properties aren't selling and get to see these first. These will be properties that have been on the market for 8 weeks or more, that may have had a few viewings, but no serious offers. It's a good tip to ask the estate agent *why* the property isn't selling, as they'll probably know and will tell you if you ask nicely – remember that they only get paid if they sell a house.

Most estate agents have a lettings arm, ask about them managing it when you've bought.

Open your eyes as to why it hasn't sold. Is it ugly? Are the vendors horrible? Or is there something more serious wrong with it? I once bought a house for way under market value because I persevered with getting access inside and paying for a structural survey on the place.

While going via estate agents is the simplest way to buy a house, the way to find a bargain is to find a motivated seller. If you find someone who wants to sell quickly then you're more likely to be able to negotiate a good price.

THINK ABOUT IT...

See all the agents in your area, especially the independents and be sure to keep an eye on sale boards going up, so you know about everything on the market.

HOW TO BUY - THE DIRECT APPROACH

If you consider yourself a shy person, don't panic, as the direct approach is not as direct as you may think.

I'm talking about posting letters or leaflets through letterboxes, offering to buy people's homes. But remember, this is a numbers game and of 100 approaches, you may only get 10 phone calls and from those calls only 1 or 2 properties that you want to see.

Some people would be discouraged by these results, but others will think that the benefit is worth the effort.

The best bit is that once you've designed the leaflet, you can sit back and wait for the calls.

But surely posting all these leaflets will take hours?

Not at all! All you need to do is to find the people who drop off the takeaway menus and cut a deal for them to deliver your leaflets too. Alternatively, you could ask the local free paper delivery person to deliver them, for a fee.

When the calls come in, you need to find out how motivated the seller is to see if there is a sufficient discount. Use the motivated seller checklist in the resources section to help you.

Then, once you're happy there's an opportunity, arrange a time to look at the property, consider the cost of any repairs and make a written offer.

As an example, I would look for a discount of at least 15%, but would complete within a month. On your tour of the property, try to establish how much they want for the house, so you know if you're in the same ball park.

This approach isn't for everyone, but it does work.

A variation on the theme is to put an advert in post office and shop windows or in the back of newspapers. There are some sample ads for you to adapt in the resources section of this book.

The paper adverts are more expensive, but they do work.

THINK ABOUT IT...

Is the direct approach for me?

HOW TO BUY - AUCTIONS

I'm sure that you'll have seen the many TV programmes where people buy property at auctions.

Some people do well and some make some stupid mistakes.

I recently met someone who'd bought a house without seeing it, even externally and he paid more for it than it was worth once done up!

There are some bargains at the auctions, but there are also some lemons and overpriced properties too.

I could write a whole book on buying at auctions but this section is meant as an introductory guide only.

The joy of auctions is that you don't have to haggle, or deal with the general public, but you do have to be able to complete within 28 days of the fall of the hammer. Some auctions even work to 14 days and if you fail to complete, the penalties are severe.

If you want to buy at auction, get to see the property, be aware of any refurbishment costs, know its market value and have the legal papers (plus any amendments to the sales particulars) checked by a solicitor.

Once you've done that, work out your ideal price and your maximum price. If you have time, offer your ideal price before the auction to see if the vendor will accept it.

Make certain though that you have funds or finance in place before you bid, as any offers made at auction are binding, unlike making an offer through an estate agent.

If you decide to bid, don't get involved too early, as your heart will start pounding. Sit back and watch where the bidding goes to.

Most auctioneers will only play 2 bidders off against each other, so don't get involved until one of them drops out.

Just make sure that the auctioneer can see you and that you don't leave it too late. Whatever you do, don't go over your maximum price!

This is a high-risk way of buying property, but one where the returns can be substantial.

THINK ABOUT IT...

Which auction houses operate in your target area? Why not visit one to see how they work?

NEGOTIATING

Again, I could write a whole section on negotiation, but this is meant as a snapshot, rather than a definitive guide.

The first tip in any negotiation is to know the value of what you want, to both yourself and to the seller.

You may think that this is the same, but it presumes you're looking at it in the same way.

Let me give you an example.

If I was looking at a 2 bed terraced house that could be converted into a 3 bed, or even a 4 bed student house, the income to me would be more than that of a 2 bed.

Alternatively, if the property needed a new boiler and bathroom, but my brother-in-law was a plumber, I get the work done for less than the vendor may expect.

The second tip is to ditch the aggressive style of negotiating.

You may think it works, but in the end you'll lose – destroying goodwill always costs money. Instead, try to find a solution that lets you both win.

I once bought a house from a woman whose children lived there and while she wanted the money, she didn't want to kick them out. So I rented it back to them. She got her cash, they still had somewhere to live and I got a ready made tenant, so we all won.

I've known purchasers attack people's decorating skills, gardening or size of house, but this doesn't put you at the top of their wish list. In fact I've known people take lower offers from people they liked. Remember this is *their* home and they're proud of it.

If you don't want to pay the asking price, it needn't be a battle, nor a problem. You can simply say that you love the house, but because of the work that needs doing/the rental income/any other reason, that it's only worth so much to you.

You could even go a step further and say that you realise that this won't be enough, so you redid you calculations a number of times.

People don't always sell to the highest bidder.

Thirdly, don't negotiate solely on price, as other things can be just as important.

For example, there are times in the year when property is harder to let (October to December), so you want the completion to tie in with these seasons.

Alternatively, you may want to delay the process in a rising market by offering a long period between exchange and completion.

Or you could ask for access, between exchange and completion, to carry out any refurbishment works or to show the property to potential tenants.

So when looking at a deal, don't focus purely on price.

THINK ABOUT IT...

Good negotiators aren't the ones who win at all costs, leaving a trail of disgruntled people in their wake, but someone who structures a deal that leaves all parties feeling like they've got a great deal.

For more practical tips and ideas why not take a look at "Bare Knuckle Negotiating" by Simon Hazeldine.

DEALING WITH TRADESMEN

Now you may be one of the lucky people, who has bought a house that doesn't need any work.

Or you may have a network of contacts that you can draw upon, who turn up like clockwork and don't charge you an arm and a leg.

For the rest of us, there are a number of tips for dealing with tradesmen.

One tip is to use the letting agent's network, as this way you're less likely to get poor service. However, some agents will charge for this, which means that it ends up costing you more.

Given that you're looking to build a property empire, it's worth taking the time to get some good contacts of your own.

Try to find yourself a handyman for the simpler jobs, as they'll be able to cover most of your day-to-day requirements, while being relatively cheap.

Don't be put off by people who charge for quotes, as they usually knock this off the bill if they are given the work. In fact, they usually give better information, as they don't need the work to pay for their time.

Most good tradesmen are booked up for at least 6 weeks, so talk to them when you're bidding on property, so that by the time you own the property, they'll be available.

Be straight about what you want them to do, when you want it doing and how long you expect it to take them. If you don't know the last point, ask them, or try to calculate it using their day rate.

Try to let them get on with the job and don't hassle them. The property will probably look like a bombsite when they're working, so if this annoys you, stay out of their way.

Don't try to haggle, saying you'll tell all your friends how good they are. Most of the good tradesmen don't need to advertise as they have plenty of work and they may be checking whether *you're* worth taking on, rather than the other way round!

Pay on time. In fact, meet the workman when he's finished the job and if you're happy with the work, pay him there and then.

If you like what they've done, tell them and make sure you don't lose their business card!

THINK ABOUT IT...

How many tradesmen do you know? Ask friends and people you trust who they recommend.

RECAP

Now we're making progress.

As you can see there are no real secrets to buying a property – just the application of a few key rules to make things go as smoothly as possible. Hopefully, you've realised that the process is much the same as buying your own home, but relies more on numbers and facts, rather than feelings and opinions.

The trick to being a successful investor is to make sure that you buy the *right* property (for your market) at the *right* price (for your strategy).

As you become more experienced, you'll get better at evaluating properties, from the perspectives of value, rental income and work required.

With your first property, you'll probably want a homebuyer's survey to make sure you don't take on any liabilities, but as you become more experienced, you may find that basic valuations are all you require.

We've looked at the various ways of buying property, from estate agents, auctions or directly from the owner and you've thought about which method would suit you.

I'd recommend that even if you decide to use an estate agent, you pick up a brochure for a local auction and go take a look. Remember that you don't have to buy, but this will give you an idea of the discounts or premiums out there.

We've also looked at the negotiation process and have talked about some tips for reducing the price, without upsetting the vendor.

Finally, we looked at tradesmen, to look at the gaps in your network and how to fill them.

As you progress up the property investment ladder, each of these skills will be honed as you look at more and more property deals.

In the next chapter, we'll go on to look at the letting process and how to get your asset to pay for itself using other people's money (OPM).

PETER STANLEY

LETTING YOUR PROPERTY

WHERE DO I START?

Ok, so you've bought your first investment property and are ready for the next step.

From your research, you'll know the market rent, the local letting agents and will have an idea as to whether there's a shortage or surplus of rental property.

You'll probably have spoken to the letting agent about their charges and they'll have courted your business.

This stage is relatively simple if you follow the basic guidelines and know what to look out for.

TENANCY AGREEMENT

Make sure that you use a 6 month AST (assured shorthold tenancy). Don't provide a longer tenancy until you know the tenant is okay.

SECURITY BOND

No matter how nice the tenant appears, always make sure that you take at least 1 month's rent as a security deposit, as well as taking the first month's rent in advance.

REFERENCES

Always play it safe and check people's references thoroughly.

NATIONAL INSURANCE NUMBERS AND PHOTO

With these bits of information, if the worst should happen, there are companies who can trace anyone, wherever they may hide. Just in case you ever need to recover outstanding rent.

INVENTORY

Make a list of the fixtures and fitting, together with comments on the condition and get the tenant to sign to confirm that they agree. Photographic evidence is particularly useful here.

MEET THEM

Even if you are using a letting agent, meet the people personally, to see if you think that they are genuine.

Don't be prejudiced against any particular type of tenant either. Young professional couples are just as likely to do a bunk as anyone else!

SHOULD I USE A LETTING AGENT?

I know that some people will have read the previous list and maybe felt overwhelmed.

While others will have read it, thought about it, worked out where they could get help and will be looking forward to it.

If you're in the first camp, there's no need to panic, as help is at hand.

For a price of between 10% and 15%, someone will handle the whole process for you. If they're really good, they'll even manage any maintenance work that's needed during the tenancy too.

Obviously, this will reduce your income, but will give you peace of mind and save you time. It's also tax deductible.

Paying someone else to do the work takes away the need to have an army of tradesmen and will help ensure that you comply with the legal requirements of being a landlord.

As a result this leaves you with more free time to either expand your portfolio or simply enjoy yourself!

When I started out, I used an agent for *all* my properties and it was only when I wanted to expand my portfolio quickly, that I started to manage my own properties.

Having said that, once I have bedded the tenants in, I usually pass them over to the letting agent.

Using a fee level of 12%, managing the properties means that 8 self managed properties gives the same income as 9 properties using a letting agent.

The best thing about using a letting agent is that their fees can be offset against the income from the property, which means the taxman is subsidising my agent's costs.

THINK ABOUT IT...

Do you want to handle all the detail yourself or are you willing to share a bit of your income for someone else to handle it?

REDUCING THE RISK

The last couple of sections may have left you worried about losing all your profits due to poor tenants.

While this is a very real risk that landlords and ladies face there are further steps you can take to limit it.

INSURANCE

You can get insurance policies to guard against problem tenants, lost income, as well as the standard building cover.

It is also possible to take out insurance against voids(periods when you don't have a tenant paying the rent), thereby ensuring a certain level of income.

INSPECTIONS

You could ask to see inside the property at regular intervals, although you run the risk of annoying the tenant if these checks are too often.

SECURITY BOND

While it's normal to take 1 month's security deposit, you could take a larger bond, although this is will make your property less attractive to potential tenants.

You could also ask to see the property if the tenant gives notice to quit, thus giving you a month to take any action if things need sorting out.

FIXTURES AND FITTINGS

Put simply, don't furnish the property and make sure that you haven't spent a lot of money on any refurbishments. Depending on your target market, furnishing a property will often not increase the rental income anyway.

As long as the property is clean, tidy and in good working order, it will let.

By keeping fixtures and fittings basic, the security bond will go a long way towards the costs of any renovation.

RELAX

While it's possible to minimise the risk, it is hard (if not impossible) to eliminate it entirely.

So, over the course of your investment career, you are likely to get at least one bad tenant. While it may be hard to swallow at the time, this is a cost of property investment – which should be offset by all the benefits.

If you are concerned about this, use a good letting agent and let them take the strain. Life's too short to worry about such things.

REQUIREMENTS

There are a number of considerations when letting a property and while this list isn't exhaustive, it covers the main points.

GAS CERTIFICATE

You must have an annual inspection by a CORGI registered plumber.

ELECTRICITY

The regulations are set to change, so that as with gas, you will need a certificate from a suitably qualified person.

INSURANCE

You must get buildings cover to cover the loan, which will also give you liability cover and you must state that the property is tenanted.

SECURITY

Even if you don't anticipate the property being empty for long periods of time, it would be worth improving the window and door security to protect against vandalism or squatters.

FIRE REGULATIONS

Make sure that any furnishings meet the latest fire regulations and fit smoke detectors as an extra precaution.

HOUSE NOT A HOME

This is one of the first rules of property investment and it can't be stressed strongly enough.

When you're doing any renovations, opt for "value for money" over "top quality", in relation to your ideal tenant. So don't spend £10,000 on a kitchen in a £70,000 2 bed terrace!

POST REDIRECTION

While there shouldn't be any post sent to the property for you, you may want to ask the postal service to redirect any post with your name on it.

FINANCE

The loan should be on a buy to let type of mortgage, rather than a homeowner kind.

While many people have used residential mortgages to fund a property investment, this severely restricts the lender's ability to take security over the property and would affect their rights if they ever wanted to take control of the property.

TENANTS - HOW DO I CHOOSE?

We need to go back to your ideal tenant and compare the applicants against your list.

We then need to make sure that the property will attract the kind of people you're after.

Then we need to decide what criteria we will compromise on. Typical examples are:

- Price
- Pet Owners
- Children
- Gardening - if applicable
- Cleaning
- Furniture - to be provided
- Availability - i.e. how long you'll wait before they move in
- Let Period - will you offer rental agreements other than 6 or 12 months
- Smokers

It's also worth finding out why they want to rent and what their history of renting is.

For example, two friends may only last 6 months before falling out, or wanting to move in with their own partners. A generalisation I know, but you can end up with one of them left in the property and unable to pay the rent.

On the issue of price, it's better to have the property full for 12 months than to take 10% more, but have to wait 2 months for it. So £450 a month, for 12 months, is £650 better than £475 for 10.

I personally don't like pets, as it can be hard to get rid of the smell after the tenant has left, but this is your house, so you get to make the rules!

THINK ABOUT IT...
What things would you be willing to compromise on?

RECAP

Hopefully, you'll now have decided whether you want to let the property yourself, or use the services of a letting agent.

You'll also know what kind of tenant would be ideal and also what areas you are happy to compromise on.

You should also have looked at a couple of ASTs (Assured Shorthold Tenancy Agreement) that you'll have picked up from local agents, made comparisons and checked which will provide you with the best cover.

Then you may have compared it to the RLA's plain English AST (see www.rla.org.uk) to see if there are any differences. You'll also know what level of security bond you'll want for the property and what period of tenancies you'll offer.

So all in all, you're ready to fill your property with tenants.

In the next chapter, we'll look at what to do once you've bought your first property and have found a tenant.

PETER STANLEY

BUILD ON YOUR SUCCESS

WHAT NOW?

So, you've read the book, applied the knowledge you've learned and bought your first investment property.

Congratulations, you're now a fully-fledged property investor!

If you want some sport then the next time that people talk about a property crash, or the curse of the property investor, ask them how many properties *they* own.

You'll soon realise that most people's knowledge comes from tabloid newspaper articles, TV programmes or someone "down the pub", which somehow makes them believe they're the font of all knowledge.

Don't worry if you're nervous, as it's to be expected when doing something new and different.

However, if you use this book as your guide and re-read sections when you need them, you'll pick up tips and ideas that you may not have noticed before.

Think of it like riding a bike. When the stabilisers come off, you need to keep pedalling to get rid of the fear of falling off but you never forget how to do it!

The good news is that the formula you've learned is now yours to keep too. You can use to make money whenever and wherever you want.

After their first purchase, some people want to sit back and see how it works out, while others will be eager to get right back out there and buy more property, now they know how easy it is.

Whichever camp you fall into, be sure to keep an eye on your first property and its locality.

Even if you're getting all you want from one property, keep watching the local market, for prices to changes in the area, so you can prepare to take advantage of opportunities or respond to threats.

THINK ABOUT IT...

Are you ready to build on your success or are you content with what you now have?

LESSONS LEARNED?

After you've bought your first property, it's wise to sit down and take stock of your progress so far.

You've taken a huge leap towards financial independence and probably undergone a radical shift in mindset.

You may also have achieved something that has seemed out of your reach for so long.

Take some time to think about what you've learnt throughout this book.

Some things to review...

- How can you strengthen your support team?

- Is your ideal tenant still the same and what might you look for in future?

- How has your knowledge of the property market grown and what can you do to keep informed?

- Are you keeping up to date details of good contacts that you've made?

- Has the journey so far been stressful and what can you do to make your next venture easier?

- How's your self confidence now?

- Would you choose a different area for future properties or are you happy to continue working where you are?

Finally, knowing what you know now, would you do everything the same way next time? If the answer to this one is yes then I'm very impressed!

These questions aren't meant to be an end of term exam, but are meant to help you look at how much you've learned since you started and to encourage you to keep on growing.

THINK ABOUT IT...

Take some time to think about what you've learned and what you'd do differently next time and write it in your journal.

THERE'S MORE IF YOU WANT IT!

Now you've learned the formula are you ready for some more?

This question is one of those that will make you fall into one of couple of camps – you can't sit on the fence with this one.

You may be raring to go and use what you've learned to continue to build your property empire. Or you may prefer to wait a while (or never do it again) because you found the whole process so stressful! If you are about done after your first investment than that's your choice, but don't rule out the possibilities. Try to establish the key factor (that made your last journey stressful) and see if there is a way of getting round it or avoiding next time?

If you are keen to buy another property then you may want to move quickly or more slowly.

There isn't a right and wrong answer here. You need to decide on a course of action that's right for you.

One thing to remember though is that you're now a professional property investor!

Unlike most people who only *talk* about buying another house, but don't want to fix toilets, deal with bad tenants or are scared of the impending property market crash, you've taken positive action and the rewards will come.

But, if you're not ready to jump back in, still keep your eye open for good opportunities and for people who want to sell quickly. Even if you're not ready to buy, you may be able to pass the lead onto someone else, for a small fee. You could also use your knowledge to look for areas that you think are undervalued now but may rise in value soon.

You don't need to take any more action unless you want to, but looking at deals will improve the quality of your decision making process when you are ready.

THINK ABOUT IT...

Have I caught the property investing bug or am I ready to take it easy for a while?

NEW AREA?

Now that you know the property investing formula and have researched an area, would you like to increase your knowledge further?

Using the same techniques that you've learned in this book you can get to know another area.

Perhaps you bought a house for capital growth and would like a second one that provides more income, or vice-versa.

Maybe, you learned some lessons with your first property, and if you had your time again, you'd do it differently.

Using the techniques you've learned, you should be able get a good feel for *any* area within a couple of hours.

For example, you can search for properties by postcode using the internet, speak to letting agents and arrange viewings for a Saturday morning, followed by a nice lunch somewhere. Property scouting can become a lucrative and enjoyable hobby that helps you to hone your analytical skills.

Hopefully, by now, you'll have caught the property investing bug and this will open your eyes to deals wherever they come up.

But don't be afraid to stick with the area you bought in.

If your property let quickly to your ideal tenant, then don't change a winning formula! Repeat it!

My personal strategy is to buy terraced houses in a couple of square miles in South & East Manchester, but if I hear of a good deal in North Manchester, I simply apply the same principles to assess the deal.

I'm simply looking for a box (in this case a house) that makes money and the house is less important than the numbers.

People seem to think that investing in property is complicated, but the process is very simple, when you know what to do.

THINK ABOUT IT...

If I had my time again, would I invest somewhere else?

SHOULD I REFINANCE?

So you've bought your first property and you paid your 15% or 20% (hopefully no more) deposit.

Hopefully after reading about the advantages of leveraging your money earlier on and the tax benefits, you didn't pay cash for the property!

Over time, the value of your property will increase, although the period of time depends largely on the fortunes of the particular area.

When the property is thought to have increased in value, some investors have the property revalued and ask the lender to provide a mortgage on the higher amount.

For example, if you bought a house for £80,000 and took out a £68,000 mortgage, you'd need a deposit of £12,000 (15%).

Now that the value has risen to £100,000, you can re-mortgage at £85,000 (85% of value), thereby repaying your original mortgage, returning your £12,000 deposit, with an additional £5,000 on top.

This effectively gives you the initial investment back as well as another £5,000 to put towards buying another property and repeating the process.

However there are pitfalls.

It will reduce your monthly profit and increase the impact of any void periods.

Depending on the lender's criteria you will typically need to be sure that the rent you're charging will cover the increased interest payments by 1.3 times in order to satisfy their requirements.

Plus, if you were to sell the property then the equity remaining may not be enough to pay the capital gains tax.

For these reasons, this process should only be used by people who are fairly financially literate. So do your numbers first and get someone with a brain like a calculator to do a sanity check!

THINK ABOUT IT...

Would I prefer to sit on my investment with less risk plan or am I willing to take a gamble by refinancing in order to grow my portfolio as quickly as possible?

FINAL RECAP - I'M HERE TO HELP

We're now at the end of this book.

In this chapter we've looked at your journey so far, the lessons you've learned and where you want to go now.

Hopefully, you've realised that there is more than one way to invest in property and what works for one person may not work for you.

Don't forget to use this book as a field guide and handbook. Dip into it whenever you want a refresher or when you are ready for your next deal.

If you have any questions about any aspects of this book on property investment then please do get in touch with me.

To your success

Peter Stanley

peter@propertymadesimple.com

ABOUT PETER STANLEY

Peter spent 15 years working in the financial services industry, where the rose to the level of corporate bank manager. Despite a number of job opportunities in other cities and countries, Peter has remained in his home town of Manchester.

Before leaving the day job, Peter spent more than 5 years researching property investment, having seen a number of colleagues and customers make money from property. After much deliberation and procrastination, he decided to take the plunge and make his first foray into the "buy to let market".

Over the last year, he has bought over 20 properties for himself and his clients and has developed a number of systems and checklists to help him minimise the amount of time that he spends on each property deal.

Learn more about Peter at his website:

www.propertymadesimple.com

PROPERTY MADE SIMPLE SERVICES

Peter offers a wide range of services, designed to help you invest in property, whether you're an absolute novice or a seasoned property investor.

His speciality is in simplifying the whole process, so that it can be done by anyone.

Peter has demystified the house buying process, designed systems to ease the burden, as well as offering one to one coaching. For those people who want to invest the minimum amount of time, Peter will find, buy, refurbish and let a property to suit their personal goals.

He also runs regular property investor surgeries, where you can have all your Property questions answered.

Allow him to personally guide you through the property investment minefield or follow his trials and tribulations of building his own property empire in his newsletter at www.propertymadesimple.com

BIBLIOGRAPHY

Blink - Malcolm Gladwell - 0713997273
Synchronicity - Joe Jaworski - 1576750310
Rich Dad, Poor Dad - Robert Kiyosaki - 0 446 67745 0
How to be Rich - J Paul Getty - 0 515 08737 8
The One Minute Millionaire - Mark Victor Hansen & Robert
Allen - 009188463 2
As a Man Thinketh - James Allen - 0 87516 0000 X
Building Wealth - Russ Whitney - 0 684 80051 9
The Richest Man in Babylon - George Clason - 0 451 20536 7
A Man's Journey to Simple Abundance - Sarah ban
Breathnach - 0 7432 0696 7
The Emyth Revisited - Michael Gerber - 0 88730 728 0
Making Money in Real Estate - 0 471 71177 2

USEFUL RESOURCES

www.upmystreet.co.uk – Find out about any area, from the nearest train station to crime statistics – all you need is a postcode.

www.multimap.com – Find any address in the UK using just a postcode.

www.rightmove.co.uk – Find properties for sale, anywhere in the country.

www.royalmail.com – After you've registered, you'll be able to find the postcode of any property in the UK.

www.eigroup.co.uk – This site will tell you about any properties that are to be auctioned, anywhere in the country.

www.landregisteronline.gov.uk – Access to the Land Registry's database for any English or Welsh property.

www.rla.org.uk – residential Landlords association

www.landlords.org.uk – National Landlords Association

www.moneyfacts.co.uk – Information on a wide range of mortgages and other financial products.

PETER STANLEY

Download your FREE 'Property Investor Tools'

For a guide to assessing how motivated a seller is, a return on investment calculator, sample advertisements for finding bargain properties, printable deal and ideal house checklists as well as a FREE newsletter complete the form at...

www.wealthaudit.com/property

BE HAPPY, MAKE MONEY

How To Turn Your Skills, Talents, Hobbies & Ideas Into Multiple Income Streams

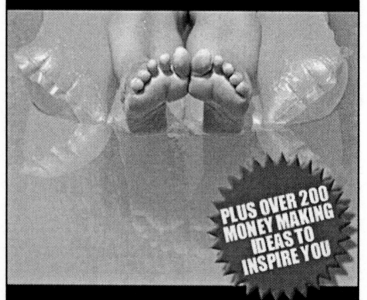

PLUS OVER 200 MONEY MAKING IDEAS TO INSPIRE YOU

JACKIE HEADLAND

www.bookshaker.com

THE S♥UL
MILLIONAIRE

True Wealth is Within Your Reach

David J Scarlett

www.bookshaker.com

THE
MONEYGYM
WEALTH BUILDING WORKOUT

WRITTEN BY TOP UK WEALTH COACH
NICOLA CAIRNCROSS

www.bookshaker.com

Printed in the United Kingdom
by Lightning Source UK Ltd.
119244UK00001B/39